OUT OF THIS WORLD

Treasured Verses

Edited By Jess Giaffreda

First published in Great Britain in 2020 by:

Young Writers
Remus House
Coltsfoot Drive
Peterborough
PE2 9BF
Telephone: 01733 890066
Website: www.youngwriters.co.uk

All Rights Reserved
Book Design by Ashley Janson
© Copyright Contributors 2020
Softback ISBN 978-1-83928-907-1

Printed and bound in the UK by BookPrintingUK
Website: www.bookprintinguk.com
YB0441K

FOREWORD

Here at Young Writers our defining aim is to promote the joys of reading and writing to children and young adults and we are committed to nurturing the creative talents of the next generation. By allowing them to see their own work in print we believe their confidence and love of creative writing will grow.

Out Of This World is our latest fantastic competition, specifically designed to encourage the writing skills of primary school children through the medium of poetry. From the high quality of entries received, it is clear that it really captured the imagination of all involved.

We are proud to present the resulting collection of poems that we are sure will amuse and inspire.

An absorbing insight into the imagination and thoughts of the young, we hope you will agree that this fantastic anthology is one to delight the whole family again and again.

CONTENTS

Jakob Grun (9)	56	Noelle Malboeuf (10)	93
Nunima Nembang (9)	57	Will Stanway (9)	94
Zak Kelly (9)	58	Felicity Cropper (10)	95
Douglas Sanger-Davies (9)	59	Megan Girish (9)	96
Megan Brown (9)	60	Jasmine Frost (10)	97
Eleanor Gould (9)	61	Michelle Chen (10)	98
Matt Docherty (8)	62	Ella Smith (9)	99
William Miles (9)	63	Harry Moore (9)	100
Henry Haywood (9)	64	Eva Landy (9)	101
Noah Rossington (8)	65	Erin Hopper (9)	102
		Calum Watson (9)	103

Frome Vale Academy, Downend

Sam Blackwell (9)	66	Cameron Bromfield (9)	104
Jaina Ellen Sarr (10)	67	Poppy Sandbach (9)	105
Endri Ahmeti (9)	68	Kaiden Barlow (9)	106
Haider Imran (8)	69	Hannah Bentley (10)	107
Jahniah Ziyan Clarence (9)	70	Isabel Frost (10)	108
Nathen Cornford Needham (9)	71	Monty King (10)	109
		Olivia Higginson (10)	110
		Amelie Axford (9)	111
		Matthew Adlam-Graham (9)	112

High Greave Junior School, Rotherham

		Harley Roscoe (10)	113
Charlie Grace Heritage (10)	72	Luca Dutton (10)	114
Niamh Murray (10)	74		

Norman Pannell Primary School, Liverpool

Victoria Burgess (10)	75	Sadie Grace Fury (9)	115
Patricija Zujeva (11)	76		
Trystan Greensmith (11)	77		

Oakington Manor Primary School, Wembley

Mossley Primary School, Congleton

		Hoorain Nisar (10)	116
Holly Webb (9)	78	Priyani Arjan (9)	118
Freya Myla Ball (10)	80	Cassidy McKeever (9)	119
Reuben Bacon (9)	82	Inaaya Raza (10)	120
Oliver Hall (9)	84	Phillipa Edwards (9)	122
Mitchell Hall (9)	85	Raheem Adanse (10)	123
Luis Arthur Statham (10)	86	Maryam Mikaiel (10)	124
Jess McCall (10)	87	Selena Zeidan (10)	125
Francesca McCarthy (10)	88	Zoya Humayun (9)	126
Gracie-Mae Thompson (9)	89	Abigail Webb (9)	127
Olivia Egan (9)	90	Aaleyah Masud (10)	128
Ezekiel Frain (10)	91	Krystalee	129
Amaya Darlington (10)	92	Chea Mills-Barnor (10)	130

THE POEMS

Off To Space

S o guess what? I'm going to space
P acking up for the amazing universe
A couple of nerves in my tummy
C ome on, let's go!
E xciting, exciting
S o off we go
H o, ho, ho! It's just like Santa in his sleigh
I go to the top of the moon!
P *op! Crackle!* goes the fire. Woohoo! Off we go!

Sophia Rabia Mitcheson (8)
Albourne CE Primary School, Albourne

My Teddy Llama

L ovely, soft and
L ovely, warm
A nice smell of lavender
M y favourite toy in the world
A darling little face.

T o hug and to tell secrets
E asy to forgive
D oes he eat grass? Yes he does
D o you have a favourite teddy?
Y ou must.

Matilda Calvert (8)
Albourne CE Primary School, Albourne

The Alien Who Was My Friend

There was an alien
Who was my friend
He drove me around the bend
He tried to make me smile
He helped me for a while
And then I named him Mile
Then he said,
"I have to go home!"
So he went
And I went back inside
And started to cry.

Charlie Solomons (8)
Albourne CE Primary School, Albourne

Planets Of Our Solar System

P lanets are great
L ovely and beautiful colours
A mazing at carrying dust
N ever miss the planets
E veryone loves to see the planets
T ell everyone in your school
S aturn is my favourite and it has cool rings.

Marli Lakhani (8)

Albourne CE Primary School, Albourne

Crack A Ring

Crack a ring
Stir the galaxy
Break a comet
Make it shine
Stroke a star
Hear it twinkle
Shake the dust
Just a little
Fly around just like that
Press it down, squeeze it flat.

Kaitlyn Cotton (8)
Albourne CE Primary School, Albourne

Horse

H elping you face your fears
O vercoming jumps
R iding by moonlight
S teep hills to ride on
E ating hay and apples.

Chloe Fender (9)

Albourne CE Primary School, Albourne

The Hottest Mars On Earth

M ars, the hottest planet!
A re we brave enough to go to Mars?
R un! The hot rocks are coming!
S ome aliens are coming!

Evie Sturt (8)

Albourne CE Primary School, Albourne

The Glowing Night Sky

G listening in the darkening sky
L ittle stars twinkle and wink
O n the horizon sits a crimson blur
W ith floating little clouds the colour pink
I n five minutes, the sky is as black as can be
N ow the full moon is bright and peeking behind the tree
G lorious stars help point north for me!

N ext, I look at the shapes made with stars
I see Andromeda, Cepheus and Draco as well
G lowing as bright as headlights of cars
H ours later, the moon has fallen
T o the west, I see a bright orange hue

S preading across the sky is a glowing white thread
K aleidoscopic colours in the sky are turning blue
Y ellow sun is up, the night has fled.

Sumayyah Ahsan (9)
Apex Primary School, Ilford

Saturn

Have you heard of Saturn?
The planet with the ring?
Well, it's not the only one with the bling.
Jupiter, Neptune and Uranus have it too.
But sorry Earth, you don't have one, I am really
sorry for you.
Now we have talked enough about rings.
So now we should actually talk about the Saturn
thing.
Did you know Saturn is 764 times the size of Earth?
But it is still second to the king.
Jupiter is 1321 times bigger than Earth.
Tough luck Saturn, hey, that rhymes with Kraken.
Saturn is so dense, it can float on water.
I bet that was something you wouldn't have
thought of.
Saturn, Neptune, Jupiter and Uranus are gas
giants.
But I do not think they will make very good places
to send your job clients!

Danyal Rashid (9)
Apex Primary School, Ilford

Solar System

S olar system is very big

O n every planet, there are various different things

L ots of people think there are aliens on Mars

A stronauts are exploring if there are actually aliens on Mars!

R obots are exploring with cameras so people can see what there is on different planets.

S o many planets in the solar system

Y et not many people can see all the planets and

S o many people want to!

T here are about a million stars in the sky

E very day, people find out new things about space!

M any astronauts have been to space from all over the world.

Yusayra Hussain (9)
Apex Primary School, Ilford

My Bunny, Twinkle

My bunny was so cool
She was lovely but hated the pool
We named her Twinkle
Because her eyes twinkled like a blue sprinkle
And a shining blue star
Her fur was softer than a car
She could jump so high
And run so fast but now makes me sigh
She left us for a new family
But we got to say goodbye.

Hibah Zikria (9)
Apex Primary School, Ilford

Ramadan

Do you see it far up high
It's a sign of night
A thread of silver shining in the dark sky
And all below they whisper prayers
Intentions made so in resolve
They do not fade
Tomorrow marks the sacred fast
Yes, Ramadan is here at last.

Inaya Gardezi (9)
Apex Primary School, Ilford

Aliens And Space

A lfie is an alien, he likes to play, he's not mean
L ennon is his second name, he likes space ball
I think he is cool like a cucumber
E veryone calls him Ant and his best friend is Dec
N o, he will not bite but he might snore loudly
S ome people think he is a robot because of how he looks

A ngry? No, but he did get angry when he lost space ball
N o one is scared of him, he is big and friendly
D o you trust Alfie or not? He might play space ball with you

S pace ball is a sport, Alfie loves space ball
P rancing Pencils is a show that Alfie likes
A lfbob is his brother, he likes space ball
C ookies are Alfie's favourite food but Alfbob doesn't like cookies
E veryone likes Alfie because he is cute and small.

Aaron Litherland (10)
Canon Sharples CE Primary School & Nursery, Whelley

My Dinner Came Alive!

I hate vegetables for my dinner and have no doubt
I will never eat one, not even a sprout!
The sweet smell of cake, oh it makes me go mad
And if I don't have a piece, I will be bad!
I hate soggy, wet vegetables and of course, the pea
It looks like the mole on Nanny McPhee!
I left the table to go and check the tele
But whilst I turned my back, something was smelly
I turned around and my food started to grow
I didn't want to get eaten, so I stayed low
My food grew a head, legs, arms and a face
They looked as hard as a mace
They hopped off my plate and swallowed me whole
Even though, to them, I was the size of a bowl
As soon as I got inside, I yelled, "Help!"
But it was no use trying, so I just shouted, "Yelp!"
After I said that, my mum saw me sitting there...
She was as angry as a bear!
I said, "Mum, I got eaten by my dinner, please believe me!"
But my mum just said, "Don't be silly!"

So to this day I'm scared of vegetables
And I will never sit back at that table
My dinner I will always fear and any vegetable
getting near.

Alfie Ellis (9)
Canon Sharples CE Primary School & Nursery, Whelley

The Spectacular Space

S uper aliens are the best, they like saving the world

P lanet Venus is a genius at acrobatics

E arth gives birth in the superspace

C raters crash to find potatoes for their tea

T im is very dim like a T-rex

A liens are very accurate at burping

C ats are very cocky to people

U p is where space is

L arry is an alien that likes to lick things

A stronauts are really good at playing ping-pong

R obby has a hobby to do.

S pace is a very clean place

P lanet Mars is a Mars bar

A stro belts are like people's belts

C ubits are like cupid

E arth is like a pear.

Harry Ritchie (10)

Canon Sharples CE Primary School & Nursery, Whelley

The School Poem

S ome schools are normal but my school is weird

C ool things at school make it feel like home

H ome is nothing like school, home is amazing

O btuse angles are pretty boring, let's be honest

O h no! I think it's almost the end of summer break!

L ook at that piece of work, it looks like a star

T ime to start learning

I can't wait for my dinner

M y eyes gaze in interest

E nough of learning, time to have some fun!

Mia Holmes (10)

Canon Sharples CE Primary School & Nursery, Whelley

The Truth About My Cat

I have a cat who wears a top hat
Her name is Belle but she doesn't smell
She has padded paws and sharp claws
Watch out! She might give you a fright at night
My cat is sometimes vicious and she can be very
suspicious
I find it sweet when she jumps on my feet
She doesn't like to swim but she goes to the gym
She likes to play in her litter tray
I guess this poem is complete
My cat is asleep dreaming about meat.

Amelia Culshaw (9)
Canon Sharples CE Primary School & Nursery, Whelley

Alien

Hi, my name is Glob
I love my family and friends
Sometimes in my cool awesome car
I turn on bends
I am very fun
When I see the sun
I am ten years old
My head is really bald
My life is not boring
My mum and dad keep snoring
I watch TV
Like my dog, Benjy
I got on a space train
And lost my brain!
I was on a tree
But it was time for my tea
That is all for my life.

Talha Anjum (10)
Canon Sharples CE Primary School & Nursery, Whelley

Favourites

F riends that play with me
A pples are red on the tree
V ans are very comfortable shoes
O ur school values are important
U K is an amazing country
R oses are very nice plants
I am having fun doing this!
T he fresh air is good
E ating grapes is great!
S ports are incredible!

Dayo Oyeyele (10)
Canon Sharples CE Primary School & Nursery, Whelley

Space Is Ace

Space is awesome
There is nothing quite like it
Super shiny stars shine bright like a diamond
Creepy aliens jump on the stars
They touch everything with their tiny arms
Space is cool
Just like a swimming pool
Oh dear!
I think I'm about to fall off a planet
That looks like an ear
Like I said, space is ace!

Lily Norburn (9)
Canon Sharples CE Primary School & Nursery, Whelley

Likes And Dislikes

L iving at home
I Phone 11 Pro
K enechi
E ating Chinese food
S inging in a choir.

D oing work
I ndian food
S inging by myself
L iving without my sister
I kea
K idney beans
E verton Football Club
S liced biscuits.

Kenechi Neo Neo Anukam (9)
Canon Sharples CE Primary School & Nursery, Whelley

The Favourites

F lappy Bird

A lan Walker's music

V ietnam holidays

O utside activities like football

U mbrellas in the rain

R ainbows

I nside activities like drawing

T eddies

E ating at McDonald's

S inging songs.

Kacper Slimak (9)

Canon Sharples CE Primary School & Nursery, Whelley

Likes And Dislikes

I like cake because it's great
I hate cabbage and I'm a savage
I like IKEA but I don't like beer
I don't like murderers
But I do like turtles
I like money
And also bunnies
I like the John Cena theme tune
I like my family
And also Christmas.

Kian Statter (10)
Canon Sharples CE Primary School & Nursery, Whelley

Dislikes

D ancing makes me mad

I hate Monday

S inging isn't my talent

L emons give me a sour face

I dislike cabbage

K iller clowns are very scary

E ggs taste funny

S prouts make me want to vomit!

Neil Hull (10)

Canon Sharples CE Primary School & Nursery, Whelley

The Day I Met An Alien!

I went into space and then I met Ace
He was an alien with a big face
We jumped from planet to planet
Oh darn it! We forgot Neptune!
Then the moon of doom came over
He said, "You need to go home!" but I moaned
So I said bye and off I flew!

Emily Ascroft (9)

Canon Sharples CE Primary School & Nursery, Whelley

A Man And His Dog Visit The Moon

S hining stars blinding my eyes
P eaceful places to roam around on
A liens roaming around on the planet
C ome on, let's get moving to the moon
E veryone's excited to see them blast off!

Noah Butterworth (10)

Canon Sharples CE Primary School & Nursery, Whelley

Likes Vs Dislikes

I don't like cats
They look like mats
I like to run
It's really fun
Spaghetti and sausages swimming around
In their nightgowns
I don't like French
It's as bad as a broken bench!

Megan Louise Gray (10)

Canon Sharples CE Primary School & Nursery, Whelley

My Likes And Dislikes

Playing with my friends
KFC is yuck!
When Christmas comes around
I can hear lots of sounds
Watching films is fun
Family is better
I wrote this poem on my own
To show my likes and dislikes.

Sienna Lloyd (9)
Canon Sharples CE Primary School & Nursery, Whelley

My Dislikes

D ays of school

I ce lollies

S prouts at Christmas

L ies that people tell me

I llnesses that I get

K FC - Kentucky Fried Chicken

E nglish at school.

Mason Smith (9)

Canon Sharples CE Primary School & Nursery, Whelley

My Likes And Dislikes

I like hot chocolate and a cup of tea
Pizza is also a favourite for me
I do not like
Fruit and cream,
Cream is the worst!
Spiders and snakes scare me to death.

Samantha Cheetham (10)
Canon Sharples CE Primary School & Nursery, Whelley

Films Are The Best!

F ascinating films
I ncredible Disney films
L ove films
M agnificent
S uper-duper films.

Lexie Carroll (9)

Canon Sharples CE Primary School & Nursery, Whelley

Australian Animals

A mazing and very cute animals
U nsuspected fires
S oon there will be no animals
T errifying fires are happening
R apidly getting worse everywhere
A nimals running for their lives
L ost animals that are actually dead
I cannot believe the devastation
A ll animals losing their lives
N ow getting injured

F rightening fires and we will hope it will stop
I f not we will be crossing our fingers
R escues in place
E vacuating the worst areas
S o many people's lives are ruined.

Gulshin Ali (9)
Clydemuir Primary School, Dalmuir

Australian Bushfires And Animals

A ll animals are going to die
U nbelievable fires are spreading everywhere
S ome people have to go into shelter
T rees are burnt down
R ight, the firefighters have to hurry up!
A ll the shelters for animals are there no more
L ike lightning they run
I s everything going to be okay?
A round Australia may be getting the fires
N ot really liking the hot fire

A ll the animals are so cute
N est building but as the trees are falling
I magine if the climate crisis had been prevented
M any lives would've been saved
A ction must be taken
L ike the weather would never compare to Scotland
S orry for anyone in Australia.

Mia Gordon (9)
Clydemuir Primary School, Dalmuir

Winter Wonderland

W ild wind, cold as ice

I cy snow as fun as sand

N ow my dog wrecked my snowman

T ime to get my warm coat on

E veryone happily playing outside

R ails are slippy, they're really dangerous

W ellies are being worn at all times

O ne of my snowman's arms fell off

N o one wearing shorts.

D ecember 25th is Christmas!

E veryone cosy and warm

R ed scarfs on everyone

L et it snow more

A lot of people warm and cosy

N ot cold and wet

D efinitely was really fun!

Adam Tarbet (9)
Clydemuir Primary School, Dalmuir

Australian Bushfires And Animals

A round the world is burning
U nbelievable fires are spreading
S ome animals have died
T iny fires spreading to big fires
R unning for safety
A n emergency declared
L ightning has started each night
I hope everyone and everything is okay
A round the world isn't on fire
N ow the fires are burning down homes

F inally it will stop
I n shelters, there are scared animals
R ed-hot fires spreading but hopefully it stops
E veryone's scared
S top please!

Abbie Macleod (9)

Clydemuir Primary School, Dalmuir

The Battle Of Time

T he end of the war was near

H ours of constant fighting

E nding with only one ship

U nited forces stood together

L oser would soon be picked

T rying so hard to not be the loser

R anked first and second in the galaxy

A nd the battle for the best rank

B attle of time

A nd resources running low

T ime was running out

T he master weapon was complete

L oser had been picked

E nd of the battle was here.

Matthew Darroch (9)

Clydemuir Primary School, Dalmuir

Australian Fires

A ll animals run in fear
U nexpecting fire grows
S ome animals are dead
T he flames are burning the wildlife
R eady to explore the forests
A nimals are dying
L ots of people are suffering, lots and lots of fires are randomly appearing
I feel sorry for Australia
A nd I hope the pain will end.

Myles Walters (9)
Clydemuir Primary School, Dalmuir

Australian Animals

A ll animals are bound to die
U nexpected fires
S preading fires all around
T rees lost
R oaming injured animals
A ll bushes on fire
L ives will never be the same
I hope it will end soon
A ll animals are hopefully safe
N ever happening again

F ires will hopefully stop
I f not, we'll be crossing our fingers
R allying together in a crisis
E vacuating the forests
S oon it will stop.

Rhys James Reilly (9)
Clydemuir Primary School, Dalmuir

Winter Wonderland

W hen winter is here we all cheer a lot
I t is the time to have a lot of fun
N ext to no one has seen snow till winter comes
T ime to get some haggis with some cold Irn-Bru
E ven though winter doesn't last too long
R ain is gone but snow is here

L ands are covered in snow
A nd winter has gone back to its cave
N ow winter is gone, we all go and pray
D ays die and come along but nothing better than winter.

Charlie Hodkinson Walsh (9)

Clydemuir Primary School, Dalmuir

A Superhero Called Danny Strong

S aturday night was dark

U nexpecting Danny walked along to his house

P eacefully he went to sleep

E xplosions outside woke him up

R eally? So much for a peaceful sleep!

H e shot out of bed to investigate

E xplosions were loud. He panicked and shouted, "Mum!" No answer

R eally, she must be at her friend's house. He got up to help

O ther people, he lifted a car to see who was in it. Who was it? It was Mum!

Ryan Logan (9)
Clydemuir Primary School, Dalmuir

Swimming

S o much beautiful blue water in the sea
W ith all of the fish swimming everywhere
I n the deep blue sea, all the colour on the coral
M oments in the sea or on the beach are so pretty
M uch more to discover in the deep blue sea
I love it when the waves pass by
N o matter where you are, swimming is free
G reat, everything is great about the water, I love the beach and the deep blue sea.

Adam McColl (9)
Clydemuir Primary School, Dalmuir

The End

S ides battle in a never-ending war
P etrifying millions in the galaxy
A fter eons of battle
C atastrophe everywhere
E vil grasping on the galaxy

B attles everywhere
A t an end it must come
T ime is about to shatter
T he final battle awaits
L ost many soldiers
E verything comes down to this
S tars win the battle with hope.

Christopher Doyle (9)
Clydemuir Primary School, Dalmuir

Winter Wonderland

W inter is here
I t's very cold
N ow we will have some hot cocoa
T he time is here, it's winter now
E verything is beautiful with snow
R ing bells every day

L and is covered with snow
A nd it is fun
N o school because of the snow
D own the hills we go!

Cameron Lane (9)
Clydemuir Primary School, Dalmuir

Australia

A nimals are dying, losing their homes

U nbelievable damage

S adly things are dying

T he wreckage

R ed-hot flames

A ll the people helping

L ost homes, hope

I t stops soon

A nd I hope the animals are okay.

Aaron Miller (9)
Clydemuir Primary School, Dalmuir

Australia

A nimals are dying
U ltimate flames are coming
S o many people injured
T rees are on fire
R escues required
A ll around
L ots of damage
I n the forest, babies are dying
A nimals are losing their babies.

Leon Stewart (9)

Clydemuir Primary School, Dalmuir

The Life Of A Turtle

I hatched out of an egg and saw the sun
I scrambled through the sand to the sea and
ensured I had lots of fun
When in the water, I had no friend
And I thought, *is this the end?*
To my surprise, something caught my eye
On further inspection, it was a turtle spy!
He asked me if I wanted to be like Bond
At first I thought I was being conned
As I swam along he asked if I needed any
information
I thought for a second and replied, "Oh yeah!" as
confirmation
My future in front of me as a spy
To catch turtle villains before they die.

Harry Tupholme (9)
Cranwell Primary School, Cranwell

The Football Fight!

Early mornings, frosty ground
Mist in the air, all around
Set up the goals, clear the pitch
No divots of grass to kill the tricks.

Tie up our laces, shinpads on tight
Red and black stripes will win our football fight
The match begins, excitement grows
Just a ball on the grass but the world at our toes!

Battle commences, win, lose or draw
A dreamer's delight, he shoots and he scores!
Brave as lions, we take on our fears
The game that's worth our blood, sweat and tears.

Ben Hutchinson (9)
Cranwell Primary School, Cranwell

Food, Food And More Food

I like to help out with the cooking
It's such fun to help Dad or Mum
We weigh and we chop, we mix up a lot
And I find it all such great fun!

I love cooking burgers, hot dogs in buns
I hate when I eat and bite my tongue
The best bit by far is when it's all cooked
Especially when the food's in my tum.

I like apples, pears and oranges
But my favourite is a hot dog
I loved my dog but she died
She ate all of the leftovers, what a greedy dog!

Eddie Hart (9)
Cranwell Primary School, Cranwell

Maths And Music

M agical multiplication mayhem
A bsolutely amazing arithmetic
T imes by infinity
H ours are not long enough
S atisfying subject

A nyone can do it
N o limit for your imagination
D on't give up and try your best

M aking music magical
U sing passion to find your way
S ounds like waves in the ocean
I will always find my way
C oming together, so let's all play.

Cameron Donnor (9)

Cranwell Primary School, Cranwell

I Feel Like A Champ When I Score

Rugby is a time to loudly cheer
Sometimes we play in a dark, cloudy storm
It rains as heavily as a waterfall
So we wrap up warm.

I sprint, I dive, I score brilliant tries
I feel like a champ when I score!
I jump high in the air
We love to run and we roar.

I've got so many friends, I can't count them
Sleaford is my team
We learn from coaches, my dad is one
To play for England is my rugby dream.

Leo Faik (9)
Cranwell Primary School, Cranwell

Gymnastics

A gymnast as graceful as a swan
Going for gold as number one

Getting up to do her routine on the floor
Doing her best and she couldn't give any more

On the bars she swung really high
On her dismount she let out a happy sigh

Before the beam she got herself ready
Because when she was on she needed to stay
steady

On the vault she landed with style
Has she won? She'll have to wait for a while.

Ruby Cumming (9)
Cranwell Primary School, Cranwell

Cats

Some cats are fluffy
Some cats are fuzzy
Some cats are fat, some cats are thin
Some like to go out, some like to stay in.

Old cats are sleepy
Young cats are leapy
Cats like fish to watch and eat
Cats have paws instead of feet.

My cats like Dreamies
And a drink that's creamy
My cats hate going to the vets
But they are the best family pets.

Grace Wainwright (9)
Cranwell Primary School, Cranwell

Subjects

S ome are good, others are bad
U sually keep me amused
B ut it's just maths that racks my brain
J ust lots of people hate good geography
E veryone is liking either literacy or maths
C areful in science, things can be highly flammable
T rouble starts in guided reading
S o today you have learnt, subjects are the worst!

Isobel Glodkowski (9)

Cranwell Primary School, Cranwell

My Guinea Pig

Autumn the guinea pig is a male
He likes to eat spinach and kale
He will often play with his toys
And he smells like stinky boys!
He has a brother called Nite
And they always fight
His colours are white, black and brown
He always makes me smile and never frown
Often he squeaks like he is talking to me
Guinea pigs are the best pets, you might agree.

Sasha Owens (9)
Cranwell Primary School, Cranwell

My Puppy, Hattie

My puppy, Hattie, so lovely and sweet
Even though she likes to bite my feet
Her face as happy as can be
And as lovely as a cup of Yorkshire Tea
She is as nibbly as can be
She pulls twigs off our redcurrant tree
She is very naughty indeed!
But she has a lighter side to her bad deeds
I love her and she loves me
This is my dog, Hattie.

Jakob Grun (9)
Cranwell Primary School, Cranwell

All About Teachers

Sometimes it's boring in classrooms I see
So let me tell you about the things you can see
Like the teachers you will see
Some are fussy
Just don't blame me!
I wonder why they get sad
Or mad
Sometimes teachers are nosy
Also dozy
Wow, I love my teachers so
Wonder why they're always so bossy.

Nunima Nembang (9)
Cranwell Primary School, Cranwell

Football Crazy

I love football
It is fun
I like to pass to everyone
But the ball
Is not tall
Even though it is small

Football's crazy
But I'm lazy
I like to kick
But I can be quick

When I score
I do a roar
I slide on my knees
Onto the floor

Goal!

Zak Kelly (9)
Cranwell Primary School, Cranwell

Friends Rule!

I like to go with my friends and play
We have so much fun, I shout, "Hooray!"
Friends are cool
They all rule
My friends are amazing
Our friendship's blazing!
Friends are cool
They all rule
My friends are the best
We never rest
Friends are cool
They all rule
Fact!

Douglas Sanger-Davies (9)
Cranwell Primary School, Cranwell

Oh Deer!

There's a mouse in my house
Which was brought in by a cat
Who sometimes sits in my hat

I saw a deer out for a stroll
Then it suddenly did a roll!
It stood up tall, what a sight!
It must have had such a fright!

There's a tiger on my street
And it ate some smelly meat.

Megan Brown (9)
Cranwell Primary School, Cranwell

My Best Friend

I love being your best friend
You will always be my friend forever
I will never be able to replace you in any way

We have our ups and downs
But they will never break our friendship
We laugh, we cry, we fight
But we will always remain friends for evermore.

Eleanor Gould (9)
Cranwell Primary School, Cranwell

Night Wonders

I want to be an astronaut
Floating above the atmosphere
Gazing at the bright stars
That shine like diamonds
In a jewellery box
Inside my helmet
The only sound is my heavy breathing
All I can touch
Is the smooth rock of the moon.

Matt Docherty (8)
Cranwell Primary School, Cranwell

The Thing

A deadly fright
A scary sight
A twisty horn
As sharp as a thorn
Long, wide wings
Like the Valley of Kings
Scales as rough as sand
Uh-oh!
Oh no!
It's a dragon!

William Miles (9)
Cranwell Primary School, Cranwell

Statue

My eye is an antique
My leg is quite unique
My tongue is made of stone
Some rocks make up my bones
And if you do break me...
They will be angry!
I'm
A
Statue.

Henry Haywood (9)
Cranwell Primary School, Cranwell

Rabbits

R abbits

A re

B eautiful

B ouncy

I nquisitive and

T ricky to catch!

Noah Rossington (8)
Cranwell Primary School, Cranwell

Life Will Live On...

At NASA HQ,
All the scientists drew
A robot that would go to space
To look for an alien race
And then at last
When it was at the launchpad
Its journey took flight
And its creators cheered with delight
Thirty-eight years later...
Voyager One is now bait
For the aliens that might come
But with only two years until his travel is done
And it's impossible with all this space-time fabric
But when the robot finds an alien planet
Which will support life
All the humans are happy that they can survive
And travel there so they can thrive.

Sam Blackwell (9)
Frome Vale Academy, Downend

Landing On Earth

I was on a mission
Brave and bold
My spaceship was ancient
Dusty and old

Suddenly, a malfunction!
I panicked and tried
As only a little girl
I began to cry

My spaceship was crash-landing
My radar said: *Earth! Danger!*
Crashed and was surrounded by men
They were wearing black suits, were they some
sort of rangers?

I was shocked, they flashed me with a light
All of a sudden, blank was my mind.

Jaina Ellen Sarr (10)
Frome Vale Academy, Downend

The Space

Space is purple and blue
That is very true
Saturn is peaceful
Well, it has no people
Do you like the sun?
Either way, it is very fun
Have you ever seen Mars?
It looks like stars
Earth is made out of land
With some sand
Seventy-five per cent of Earth is seas
The other twenty-five per cent is trees
Space is a place
Without a face.

Endri Ahmeti (9)
Frome Vale Academy, Downend

The Brave Man

Once there was a man
Who got lost in space
He was thinking what to do
He saw an alien, he got scared
He shot a missile, what could he do?
He smashed down on Earth
He told everyone but no one believed him
He was in bed but an alien was in his spaceship
Then he got killed.

Haider Imran (8)
Frome Vale Academy, Downend

Moon Lady

Moon Lady
What do you do?
On the eerie, big, massive moon?
Do you bing?
Do you bong?
Do you rattle all day long?
Do you climb?
Do you fly?
So you draw a big smile?
Do you laugh?
Do you giggle?
What do you do?
Moon Lady, who are you?

Jahniah Ziyan Clarence (9)
Frome Vale Academy, Downend

The Space...

There was an alien
And the alien met a famous person
Called Neil Armstrong
And then he said hello
And the alien said that was the first person
To say hello to him
And the alien said,
"Are you on TV?
Are you famous?"
He said yes.

Nathen Cornford Needham (9)
Frome Vale Academy, Downend

My Magical Little Brother

I have an amazing little brother
Who is out of this world
And here are the reasons why...

He has amazing eyes
And an infectious smile
His laugh is contagious
And he will melt your heart from the start

He struggles with his knowledge
But it's not his fault
He tries his best
All the time

He likes to dance and jump around
But that's his way
Of having fun

He may not understand
What is going on
But he still takes part
In what he can

People may point and laugh at him
But that's my brother
He is one special
Down Syndrome kid

I love him to bits
I couldn't live without him
He's my little brother
And also my little star.

Charlie Grace Heritage (10)

High Greave Junior School, Rotherham

Star Wars

In a galaxy far, far away
On the ship sat Luke and Rey
Examining an alien they had just found
On the planet Belsavis, not far off the ground
"What shall we go?" Luke asked Rey
"I don't know," she said, "but keep it away!"
The alien yawned and lay down its head
Shut its eyes and slept and slept
Luke shrugged and sat at the wheel
Where he pressed some buttons made of steel
Off they went, as fast as lightning
Some would have thought it was a little frightening
But Luke and Rey were the bravest in the land
They looked at one another and shook each
other's hand.

Niamh Murray (10)
High Greave Junior School, Rotherham

Darkness

Out of this world, in the middle of space
Lies a whole world of darkness and nothing could
be placed
Apart from the stars that shone upon the planet
Where lived an animal
Who went by the name of Janet
Janet was strange and out of this world
With a face with three eyes and hair that was
curled
Janet was pointy but gentle to touch
With a voice that was so soft and gentle as such
All she wanted from out of this world
Was a lot less darkness and a whole new world.

Victoria Burgess (10)
High Greave Junior School, Rotherham

Space Cat

He zooms by like lightning
He isn't afraid
Even if there are aliens!
He lands on the moon
He is greeted by green things
They are frightening!

Space Cat wants to go back to Earth
But something out of the ordinary happens
The green things stole his spaceship
He's not Space Cat anymore
He's Stranded Cat now...
Why, why, why?
As he sulks in shame.

Patricija Zujeva (11)
High Greave Junior School, Rotherham

Galaxies Of Galaxies

Far, far away
In a galaxy we do not know of today
I wonder if there are children at play?
A boy like me
A girl like Emily
Staring at the stars
Maybe they live on Mars
Playing the same game
Or having the same names.

Trystan Greensmith (11)
High Greave Junior School, Rotherham

It Belongs In The Sky, Not Your Jar!

Jeff and Bob looked out at the night sky
Bob noticed a bright star and wondered why
It shone so bright
In the cold, frosty night
Jeff said, "Let's see if we can reach the star!"
Bob whispered, "No way, it is too far!"
"Don't be daft, Bob, come and see my invention!
It's my new rocket as fast as lightning, and it's my intention
To soar up high and land on the moon
So we can get a better view of the star very soon!"
It will not take long, no time to waste!"
They jumped in the rocket and blasted into space
In less than a minute, they arrived on the moon
Jeff looked up at the star, so bright
Shining like silver in the night
He stretched up high
To pick it out of the sky
And put it in his jar
But it suddenly went dark

And the sky went pitch-black
"Quick, Jeff! Put it back!" shouted Bob
"It's way too gloomy without the star!
It belongs in the sky, not your jar!"
So Jeff placed it back into the night sky
To light their way home
Back in the rocket, at the speed of light
They rushed back to Earth at the dead of night
"Wow! That was an adventure
But now it is time for bed
I am tired and I need to rest my head!"

Holly Webb (9)

Mossley Primary School, Congleton

Daydream

Imagine climbing high, I'm almost there,
I look around, I've left the ground,
In front of me are stars but no cars,
Shining bright, but there's no light; it's all a delight,
I feel excitement, I want to scream,
Is it all a daydream?

Suddenly, a mysterious light shone, what was I
standing on?
Could it be a shooting star? Off I go so very far.
Faster and faster through the sky, how was I up so
high?
Above the castles, skyscrapers and towers, I can
barely see the flowers,
Higher and higher I go, up into space,
Can I really be travelling at such a pace?

When will this end? I want to go home, I feel so
alone,
A wave of panic sweeps over me, will I ever be
free?
I close my eyes, will this be my demise?
I am falling, falling to the ground,

It all seems clearer now; I can hear a sound,
It's warm and sunny and the birds are singing, I
can hear the children giggling,
I open my eyes, I feel safe and secure,
I am back on Earth after a quick detour.
It was a daydream after all!

Freya Myla Ball (10)

Mossley Primary School, Congleton

My Space Journey

As I leave Earth's atmosphere,
Which feels like a protective boundary,
Silent but radiant stars sprint by,
I hear the rhythmic throbbing of the spaceship's engines
As we hurtle along at light speed
To our destinations.

I watch in wonder
As giant marvellous planets whizz by.
Oh look!
There is Venus,
Third brightest in the night-time sky,
Mars, so red
It looks like a giant cherry in the sky.

Then Jupiter,
A giant hiding behind gas and dust
And Saturn with her rings of ice
Which would freeze me to stone
In a flash.

Uranus, the chilly undisputed ice giant
And Neptune, the oldest of them all.

But wow,
Oh no,
Time to go,
To leave this wondrous place.
As Earth comes slowly into view
With comforting emerald and cobalt blue
Candyfloss cotton clouds,
I think how she gives so much.

So close to home,
I realise we must never take our beautiful planet
for granted.

Reuben Bacon (9)

Mossley Primary School, Congleton

Down The Ramp!

One sunny morning, there on a messy bed slept a snoring chatterbox named Slappy. He wasn't like everyone else, he was a fearless skater who dreamed of skate parks. There was one thing that he was scared of, the mega ramp. It went up for twenty metres and was very very steep! He got his gear on and off he went down the road to the mega ramp. As he climbed up lots and lots of steep steps onto the top ramp, he remembered the pain of his broken leg on his first ever attempt but it didn't stop him. He reached the top, took two deep breaths, closed his eyes and down he went! At the end of the ramp, he felt his wheels come off the floor and for a moment he forgot about everything. He hit the kicker jump, pulled off some tricks and landed it!

It was then when he was woken by his alarm for school... Had it all been a dream...?

Oliver Hall (9)

Mossley Primary School, Congleton

To The Moon!

Deep down in a space station, flew an elf called
Steve. His dream was to walk on the moon. Today
was the day his dream was going to come true. He
was excited and ready for action. *Ten, nine, eight,
seven, six, five, four, three, two, one...* Blast-off!
The rocket flew like a bird. He closed his eyes and
a moment later, he was in space. He could not see
a thing except for the shiny, glimmering moon.
The rocket captain Buzz, who was a space expert,
said, "we have landed and It is time to step on the
moon!"
They rushed to get their spacesuits on, walked to
the rocket's door, jumped and took their first steps.
"Yay!" shouted Steve. "I did it!"
He put the Elf flag on the moon and went back
home to tell everyone on the space station about
his adventure.

Mitchell Hall (9)
Mossley Primary School, Congleton

Out Of This World

The sparkling sun, a burning ball of fire
Gives life to Earth with great desire
Miniature Mercury, speeds around the sun
Whizzing round and round like a ball of fun
Vigorous Venus, the goddess of love
Has a rocky surface up above
Extraordinary Earth, full of wonderful life
Human pollution and climate change causing strife
Marvellous Mars, orange and red
Deep craters and colossal mountains above our heads
Gigantic Jupiter, full of gas
Bigger than any other planet with a very large mass
Super Saturn, surrounded by rings
Stretching out into space, spreading its wings
Unique Uranus, rolling on its side
His blue-green haze does not like to hide
Nippy Neptune, last in the line
Swirling storms and extreme weather both combine.

Luis Arthur Statham (10)

Mossley Primary School, Congleton

Earth

One early morning on Planet Mars, we spied a
nearby planet
Where all is familiar indeed
On this ginormous, circular planet,
We saw seas and continents, blue and green all
over it
We spied brown and green things sticking out of
the ground
Nutritious red, round things were on them like glue
We wondered what they were
And kept looking
We soon found objects made out of big, long
rectangles called bricks
It was pointed outside with humans roaming
around like soldiers
We also found things of every colour
Rapidly zooming along roads like headless
chickens
People were inside chatting away
We dreamt of visiting the planet
But we were never able to
So we named it Earth.

Jess McCall (10)
Mossley Primary School, Congleton

Out Of This World

Out of this world is a colossal rainbow spinning
around and skimming the Earth's surface
Out of this world are perilous dinosaurs bounding
to each planet with their sharp, deadly claws
scraping the cities to space
Out of this world are different cake layers, each
protecting the Earth for their own reasons
Out of this world are giants floating upside down,
kicking from planet to planet
Out of this world are volcanoes erupting insecure
to the ground with no gravity at all
Out of this world are unicorns floating with their
horn pointing first, making ditches in the earth
every millisecond
And this is how I imagine the world is on the
outside.

Francesca McCarthy (10)
Mossley Primary School, Congleton

Stars At Night

Stars, stars, shining bright
Flickering in the sky at night
Up above, down below
The stars are gleaming like snow.

Moon, moon, shining bright
Underneath the clouds at night
The dazzling, molten moon
Circling the Earth with its special tune.

Shadows of the nocturnal animals show
The bats burst out like flashing fireworks
Foxes foraging like fierce warriors
Whilst the stars and moon lead their way.

Moon and sun swap faces
Stars and clouds change places
As night turns to day
It's now time to explore and play.

Gracie-Mae Thompson (9)
Mossley Primary School, Congleton

Amazing Aliens

As the stars glimmered and the moon thoroughly spread light, the sunrise awoke and the moon disappeared. The stars were like an ocean waiting to be discovered. So as the aliens whispered, the spaceships shouted in laughter. The aliens smiled in astonishment. The spaceships growled as the shining sun arose. The planets crunched together as Mars screamed at the burning, scorching sun and as Jupiter met his demise. The magical aliens cried till they were like a river surfing over a canal. The mythical, natural hot sun burnt the aliens' backs as they came out of their shells.

Olivia Egan (9)

Mossley Primary School, Congleton

The Scorpion, The Skull, The Snake

The Scorpion stings, the Skull lies, the Snake slithers

In space, they sting, lie and slither
In space, they live
In space, they die
Where death is daily
Where life is a miracle.

The Scorpion stings, the Skull lies, the Snake slithers

Together, the Scorpion, the Skull and the Snake can defeat Zeus, King of Gods
In space, Zeus lives
In space, Zeus dies
In space, the Scorpion, the Skull, the Snake live
In space, the Scorpion, the Skull, the Snake die.

The Scorpion, the Skull, the Snake.

Ezekiel Frain (10)
Mossley Primary School, Congleton

My Adventures Of Space!

Space is a mysterious place
Like a darkened room or an unknown face
Space is scary, fascinating and vast
Could any living thing ever last?
Space is somewhere I am keen to explore
I just want to find out more and more!
Space is exquisite, I wonder what else we can see
If we visited one day, maybe we would see an alien
or three!

Maybe one day I'll get there soon
Like Neil Armstrong who landed on the moon
Maybe one day I will see the courageous
astronauts soon
What an amazing thought that may be.

Amaya Darlington (10)
Mossley Primary School, Congleton

The Loving, Magical Times

Going outside to play
Is something everybody likes to do all day
But beyond the waterfalls and across seas
Are rainbows, fairies and unicorns maybe
Wishes and dreams are stuff here
They probably do it all day here
Fairies are very talented
Although you might know that
Pegasuses fly over the moon
And you might see them soon
Rainbows stretch to Dreamland
Where animals eat some of its fertile land
This is my story
Where it's above and beyond your wildest dreams.

Noelle Malboeuf (10)
Mossley Primary School, Congleton

A Race Through The Woods

He raced as the murky, dull water beside him was stagnant. A twist and a turn took him to the dark and gloomy woods. The overgrown trees lurched over us as we frantically strode to the clearing. Golfball-sized hailstones pelted us. The dog tried to catch the hailstones, thinking they were his tennis balls. As the wind blew, the dog spun faster and faster until he caught up with his own tail. Dizzy with excitement, he chased the falling hailstones until his legs felt like wibbly wobbly jelly. Would the dog make it home?

Will Stanway (9)
Mossley Primary School, Congleton

Breathtaking Aliens

As the breathtaking aliens emerge from their
homes
The planets orbit the world.
Spaceships land on the admirable, intriguing
planets Venus and Mars.
These amazing aliens wander around skipping and
playing
In and out the asteroids that fly past like a
shooting star.
Their eyes sparkle in the light of the moon,
They all have magical, unique things about them.
These beautiful creatures come in all shapes and
sizes
That become the outstanding, breathtaking aliens.

Felicity Cropper (10)
Mossley Primary School, Congleton

The Planets And Stars...

The stars swiftly fly past the planets
As a trail of wonder flies past
The mysterious planets wonder
As the mystical trail of wonder flies past

The giant, colossal planets circle the sun
As the stars surround the milk planets
There's a quiet silence... as light appears
It's the magical trail!

Once again, the solar system
Is enchantedly filled with life and love
All thanks to the planets and stars.

Megan Girish (9)
Mossley Primary School, Congleton

The Night

The darkness encases me like a harsh blanket
I hear the clicking of tap dancers on the firm,
freezing floor
I close my tired, weak eyes tightly to hide what I
think I saw
As I see the shadows dancing joyously
I fear I may not be alone in my gloomy, dark room
The malevolent, brutal shadow's voices start
shouting, "It is real life!" at me
Without warning, I hear the familiar sounds of
home
And realise it was all a dream.

Jasmine Frost (10)
Mossley Primary School, Congleton

Alarming Aliens And Radioactive Robots

Screaming, shouting,
Fighting furiously.
In the blink of an eye
Numerous amounts of grotesque, perilous
creatures appeared.
Ridiculously, the foolish horrific monsters were
Annoyed.
Offended, the gloopy green-looking
Terrifying aliens
Spat gloop everywhere!
The radioactive robots - who were frequently ready
Had an unexpected jagged tooth.
Will the mythical creatures ever make peace with
each other?

Michelle Chen (10)

Mossley Primary School, Congleton

Cleo The Cat

Cleo the cat, is her name
Chasing mice, is her game
In the field, she will wander
Where to go, she will ponder.

To the neighbours, she will go
With one beady eye, on that crow
Squawk! Squawk! the crow will screech
To the tall oak tree, he will reach.

After that, it's time to rest
Catnapping for hours, seems the best
On the bed, she will lay
Until the children, come back to play.

Ella Smith (9)
Mossley Primary School, Congleton

Moon Madness

O n the moon we stood
U ntil an alien came along
T hree actually

O ur hearts stopped
F or a second

T hey approached
"H elp!"
I
S creamed

W ithout warning
O ne of the aliens
R andomly started to dance
L aughter followed, mine and theirs
D id we make some friends?

Harry Moore (9)
Mossley Primary School, Congleton

Curious Koalas

Curious koalas hang in overgrown trees
But they have extremely crinkly knees
Sometimes they have food in their bellies
But you definitely can't feed them jelly
Their poo can be very smelly
But not as smelly as a damp welly
They love to eat bamboo
But at least they don't eat their poo
Sometimes they eat people's shoes
But if they are in a race, they would more than
likely lose.

Eva Landy (9)
Mossley Primary School, Congleton

The Miraculous Milky Way

Hot dust making stars
The Aurora Borealis
The Earth's magnetic field trapping in oxygen and gravity
Jupiter, Saturn, Venus and Mars.

Anonymous aliens
The magnificent Milky Way
The scorching sun blazing down on Earth
Ginormous Jupiter.

The Milky Way is a glorious galaxy
Spreading out for light-years
Like Nutella on a toasty sky
With Smarties as stars.

Erin Hopper (9)
Mossley Primary School, Congleton

In Space

Bright stars glimmer
Whilst the dark space sleeps.
The planets,
Which are very far away,
Are gigantic.
Deafening, scary black holes
Devour everything that approaches them.
Planets circle round the beautiful blazing sun.
The multicoloured Northern Lights
Pattern the outside of the Earth.
The ISS,
Which carries astronauts,
Is also a science laboratory.

Calum Watson (9)
Mossley Primary School, Congleton

First Moon Landing

T here were 600 million people holding their breath

H istory being made with one small step

E xcited children dressed up as spacemen

M iles above Earth, they risked their lives

O ne wrong move could cause disaster

O uter space, a brand-new chapter

N eil Armstrong, Buzz Aldrin and Michael Collins. Their names were never forgotten.

Cameron Bromfield (9)

Mossley Primary School, Congleton

A Little Crazy Outer Space!

Space is ace, it's a wonderful place
See Mars, Jupiter and Saturn, they're always in a race

Mars always on the inside track
It has the shortest year of the three in the pack

Jupiter with its massive storms
It's a gas giant and could devour us all

And distant Saturn with its beautiful rings
A sight to behold that will make your heart sing.

Poppy Sandbach (9)
Mossley Primary School, Congleton

Aliens

These are aliens, they are friends with the
Transylvanians
Some aliens come from Mars
But instead of driving cars
They go around in monster trucks
And they all think that working sucks
Some aliens live on the moon
If there's food around, they'll be there soon
They are all pretty weird
Because they don't wear socks
And they like to eat moon rocks.

Kaiden Barlow (9)
Mossley Primary School, Congleton

Up And Away In Space!

Bang! As the shooting stars go by
High up in the dark night sky
The sun is blazing up in space
No planet is out of place.

Up in space, I have unimaginable grace
Although I move at a snail's pace.

My home is down below
But the stars have a tempting glow
It makes me want to stay in space
High above the human race.

Hannah Bentley (10)
Mossley Primary School, Congleton

My Fishing Life!

Here I go with my rod and line
Treading in the murky, messy mud, yet taking my
time
Sitting by the crystal-clear waters
I look up at the dazzling sun
I'm looking forward to having some fun
As the bait sings out, "Hello!"
The fish come from the depths below
As my float sails away just in time
Oh how I love fishing, it is fine.

Isabel Frost (10)
Mossley Primary School, Congleton

Splashtastic

I swim hungrily like a shark
It's not a walk in the park
Training daily keeps me happy and fit

Other days I am a dolphin
Chasing the gala win
It's not all about the medals of course

The water feels icy-cold
At least it helps me win a gold
Afterwards, a deep sleep feels good.

Monty King (10)
Mossley Primary School, Congleton

Happy Times

The grass is green
The sky is blue
Sing all the way
Happy aren't you?
Sharing stories
Here comes Roary
Never know how
Long we will be
Now it is time
To go to sleep
Wakey-wakey
Aren't you nine?
Because I thought
It was the end of our time.

Olivia Higginson (10)
Mossley Primary School, Congleton

Vicious Volcano

The dozing volcano woke up with a grumble
A cough, a splutter, en eruption, a rumble
The blazing hot lava came spewing out
The surrounding, petrified villagers began to shout
The flaming red and orange ooze came bubbling down
Once it settled, it turned black on the ground.

Amelie Axford (9)
Mossley Primary School, Congleton

The Donkey On The Moon

There was a donkey on the moon
And as he gazed around
All he could see were stars above
And there wasn't a single sound.

There was a donkey on the moon
He loved the sparkling stars
But then became very hungry
And ate some chocolate bars.

Matthew Adlam-Graham (9)
Mossley Primary School, Congleton

A Slow Sloth

A sloth lives in a tree
And it is its favourite place to be
It usually sleeps
And it keeps its place in the same tree
And then it will get up and eat a pea
And then it will go and be a slow sloth over and
over again.

Harley Roscoe (10)
Mossley Primary School, Congleton

Nature On Mars

Nature is important to life
But on Mars, no one has ever heard of or seen
nature
But there is some nature on Mars
There is rich sand and some dead trees
Remember, nature is important.

Luca Dutton (10)
Mossley Primary School, Congleton

Planet Travel

There are many planets in our solar system and
our space,
But the best one is our moon with its shiny, smiling
face.
It's got lots of craters and lots of holes,
It looks like it's been invaded by a massive army of
moles.

We want to go to Jupiter,
But I think it might make us stupider!
Anyway, I think it'll take a year
And I'd shake with fear.

I'd like to go to the Milky Way
And I would make milky people pay on the way!

Sadie Grace Fury (9)

Norman Pannell Primary School, Liverpool

The Dying Planet

This planet that we live on
Has been around for thousands of years,
But prepare your ears,
The event that creates fears
Is unfolding before your eyes.

The rainforests are burning,
It is quite concerning,
I am a pluviophile,
I adore the rain,
Don't worry, I am sane.

But how do I enjoy the rain
When the Earth is literally in pain?
The beautiful blue sky sure is idyllic,
The alluring clouds may seem angelic

But thick black soot smoke rises from the top of
factories,
My asthma finds it unsatisfactory,
Coughing people, dying people,
All the cause of 'just a few' chemicals.

Haven't we all experienced the serendipity of help
Arriving unexpectedly when we need it?
When will the Earth experience it?
If you think about it, we're all basically murderers
Of our Earth.

This doesn't only occur on land either,
Clear oceans are now filled with plastic,
No point for you to be sarcastic,
What have innocent sea creatures ever done to
you?

Plastic.
The main word is plastic,
You might say I'm being dramatic,
But you'll remember me when the Earth is as hot
as your kitchen stove.

Although most people don't really care,
Some people agree that this is not fair,
It gives me euphoria to see,
That some people want to stop this, like me.

Save the Earth!

Hoorain Nisar (10)
Oakington Manor Primary School, Wembley

Monsters

Monsters, monsters, they come in the night,
Monsters, monsters, they give you a fright.
Monsters, monsters under the bed,
Monsters, monsters, you're afraid they will bite off
your head.
Monsters, monsters, they are quite scary,
Monsters, monsters, some of them are quite hairy.
Monsters, monsters, in the dark they lurk,
Monsters, monsters, they greet you with a smirk.
Monsters, monsters, they will eat your liver,
Monsters, monsters, they will make you shiver.
Monsters, monsters, they will nibble at your feet,
Monsters, monsters, they are not pleasant to meet.
Monsters, monsters, I've seen you before,
Monsters, monsters, some of you are still knocking
at my door.
Monsters, monsters, I promise you I won't be
scared,
Because now I'm really prepared!

Priyani Arjan (9)
Oakington Manor Primary School, Wembley

The Space Aliens!

Angelica had been training for this moment for
most of her life,
Now, sitting strapped to a spaceship, you could cut
the tension with a knife.
Her heart was beating as fast as a drum,
Her mouth salivating as if she had chewed gum.
"Five, four, three, two, one... blast-off!" the
controller announced,
The gum floated from her mouth and bounced.
Angelica and her crew began floating in the air,
Suddenly, the ship began rocking and there was a
huge bright flair.
Looking out the window, Angelica could see
An alien ship and the aliens were fat, in green!
"All hands on deck, we're under attack!"
We blasted our biggest rocket and the sky turned
black.
We had killed the enemies, our mission was
complete,
My heart no longer sounded like a drum beat.

Cassidy McKeever (9)
Oakington Manor Primary School, Wembley

Sights And Beyond

As the glistening stars shine in the flickering
moonlight,
Phenomenal things happen beyond the immense
darkness.
Stars hang on the curtain draped across the
exquisite night sky,
The glint of light from the clear moon spotted by
life below.

Mysterious floating planets orbiting the glorious
sun,
Shooting stars racing through the midnight air.
Miraculous sights appear for all living creatures,
Although there is, for a fact, way more beauty than
that.

The stars, the moon, the sun, the planets,
What could be more spectacular than the outer
world?
So many alluring sights to see,
So many more things to know.

Now the beauty of space and its wondrous things
are revealed,
Everything and anything that is found in the galaxy
is out of this world.

Inaaya Raza (10)

Oakington Manor Primary School, Wembley

Alien Invasion

Bang, crash, thud!
What on earth was that?
Nobody knew if they would face their dreaded fear
The light was shining as bright as the sun
What would all the amazing humans become?
The sapphire-blue sea; what would it do to me?
Whatever landed on Earth, would it be able to kill me?
Slimy green creatures stepped out of the spaceship
I couldn't believe everybody's surprised faces
Speaking a gibberish language nobody could understand
Why don't the scientists have a plan?
Tick-tock, time is ticking, we don't have a plan
Could aliens take over the world?

Phillipa Edwards (9)
Oakington Manor Primary School, Wembley

Intergalactic Wars

The time was 3:30pm and the school bell rang, my walking pace turned into sprinting. As quick as a thought, a giant hole started to appear. I fell in with an enormous bang!

I opened my eyes and I was in the car of an alien. In the background, I could hear deafening laser gunfire travelling at rapid speeds and tanks with powerful cannons! I thought that humans were the only beings who'd developed this tech but it turns out robots are intelligent like humans. These radical robots were fighting an opponent they didn't know. The aliens' knowledge about robots was starting to grow...

Raheem Adanse (10)
Oakington Manor Primary School, Wembley

Here Come Spiders

Beep beep! I hear a noise,
As it goes crashing down dust,
Waves striking in and out.
What a drought!
Here comes some more, argh!
Sand sinking in through our feet,
This is not a great beat.
Low murmuring of little peeps
And now a rockslide comes in.
Crash! We're all smashed!
Now how do we fix this mash?
Wait! I hear the noise of huge feet,
The path opens wider
And here comes spiders!
Will he fix this
Or will he be behind bars?
Argh! Watch out,
Here comes a waterfall!

Maryam Mikaiel (10)
Oakington Manor Primary School, Wembley

The Alien Duck

I know a Selena
Living in a space arena
With her mum, dad and sister Sabrina.

An alien duck she is,
Full of energy, the little miss,
When she's happy,
She goes all whizz.

On the ring of Saturn,
Where everything is a pattern,
Selena learnt Latin.

In the early morning,
She's always talking
And trying to be like Stephen Hawkins.

And that's our friend in space,
Full of ever so much grace,
Who we will never be able to replace.

Selena Zeidan (10)
Oakington Manor Primary School, Wembley

Our Gorgeous Galaxy

I want to invite the stars for a walk,
If only we could talk,
Before we make our way to the gorgeous galaxy
And see the lovely solar system.

I love the galaxy,
The way it leads past eternal dark.
The different colours that mix together,
What lovely colours to create our Milky Way.

I love the galaxy,
I love its light,
Oh, how the stars twinkle so bright.
The way it leads past eternal dark.
It truly is as wonderful as a Christmas present!

Zoya Humayun (9)
Oakington Manor Primary School, Wembley

Lost In Space

After I went to go play
I decided to call it a day
When I took a nap
I realised I was falling in a trap
I did not know where I was going to go next...

Bam! I was surrounded by stars
And I found the planet Mars
I couldn't believe my eyes
And I didn't even get to say my goodbyes

Then I found out it was just a dream
Thank goodness I didn't get hit by a large alien beam
But space will always be in my head, you see...

Abigail Webb (9)
Oakington Manor Primary School, Wembley

Alex The Alien

A lex is an alien,
L exi is his best friend
E xtra intelligent is what he is
X ylophone is his favourite instrument

T he spaceship is his favourite car
H e never leaves anyone out
E ats what he is served

A s fast as a cheetah he runs
I s half human and half alien
I t's never a new Alex
E ach day we will check on him
N ow we will see you later, Alex!

Aaleyah Masud (10)
Oakington Manor Primary School, Wembley

The Planet In Space

The planet is red
It's very far ahead
For technology.
It has two moons
With long afternoons.

It has a ring
Until the Earth season turns to spring.
The planet is twice as nice
And gives people better advice
For being spectacular on a good device.

The planet is kind
And has a lovely mind.
It can turn orange when people set off in space
And when they're in the rocket, they play a pack of
cards with no ace.

Krystalee

Oakington Manor Primary School, Wembley

Man On The Moon

The man on the moon was not scared for the
journey ahead,
He was ready and prepared to get out of bed.

As he climbed into the rocket,
He gave a big smile.
Everyone waved 'cause he wouldn't be back in a
while.

He flew around the planets: Jupiter, Saturn and
Neptune.
Then came back to the moon and landed quite
soon.

He had a short time left before he went back
home.
Then landed on Earth with a piece of white stone!

Chea Mills-Barnor (10)

Oakington Manor Primary School, Wembley

Planet Blop!

A liens, slimy!

L ittle round blobs.

I f you dare to,

E ntertain them...

N oisy, deafening,

S quealing, shrieking, slimy!

O n another planet they exist,

N ot a holiday destination on your wish list.

B lop is its name,

L ime or yellow?

O range or red? I guess it's all the same.

P lanet Blop - not for the sane.

Come if you dare!

Anjali Sharma (10)
Oakington Manor Primary School, Wembley

Out Of This Planet

Here I am, out of this planet,
I don't know why I have a bonnet!
I am unsure of how I got here,
Sometimes I think to myself that I need to get off this planet.
Well today, somehow, my wish came true,
I am not sure which planet I am on,
I am really anxious because there could be aliens here,
Watching me at this very moment.
I am going to close my eyes
And see if I go back to my home planet...

Iqra Ismail (9)
Oakington Manor Primary School, Wembley

Sneaky Aliens Is What They Are

S neaky aliens is what they are
P ranking people is what they do!
A rtistic is what they are
C atering is what they do
E xcellent is what they are.

A dorable is what they are
L ying is what they do
I ntelligent is what they are
E ggs are what they eat
N umber bonds is what they learn
S uper is what they are.

Jahzaiah Sowah-Cunningham (9)
Oakington Manor Primary School, Wembley

Cartoon World

Once, there was an unknown cartoon world,
So beautiful, so marvellous,
But it showed a bit of laziness,
The sky was filled, enigmatic

A bit too dramatic,
Filled with superheroes,
No villain to be afraid of,
No dying to be seen

Not like other planets,
But similar to cartoons on TV.
It's a little bit weird,
And they didn't know about fruit like kiwi!

Khusal Bariya (10)

Oakington Manor Primary School, Wembley

I Can Change Into Anything!

As fast as lightning,
I can change into anything,
I can be the thing
That you are holding!

I can be a hat,
Or maybe a cat,
Even a bat
And a pink rat!

I can be the mouse
Living in your house,
I can be your hamster
That you so like to pamper!

I can be anything,
I can be something
That you are holding,
I can be anything!

Anna Kastrati Kristofova (10)
Oakington Manor Primary School, Wembley

The Great Dad Rescue

A dad wanted his son to come with him
The son said no and wanted to go out with Tim
They both went to space and didn't go back
The dad played with his son with a sack
The dad drifted out into space
While his son had to save him
They both returned to Earth safe and sound
The dad wanted to play with him and flipped a pound
The son won and gave himself a clap!

Tyra Jules (10)
Oakington Manor Primary School, Wembley

The Luminous Expanse

Always it is lightless
Looking to the sky
But suddenly up in the vast
A star is shining bright

I fly up into the air
Towards the blazing sun
Hotter than the hottest fire
There since time had begun

The black turns into neon purple
A luminous expanse
The frozen gloom around me turns
Into an otherworldly dance...

Adam Sefsouf (9)
Oakington Manor Primary School, Wembley

I'm A Panda

If you ever go to China
Look out for black and white
I'll be climbing up a tree
I'm a real rare sight!

I'm a little shy
And love eating bamboo
Take care of my habitat
As I sit here and chew.

I need the trees to climb
I need bamboo to eat
My species is too precious
To accept defeat!

Eden Renaud (10)
Oakington Manor Primary School, Wembley

Intergalactic Galaxies

Comets fly here and there
And galaxies are everywhere.
Cosmic dust waves around Venus.
Outer space can be seen from Earth.
Stars twinkle in the night sky like fairies.
Saturn, Mars, Jupiter, Uranus, the moon, the sun
Float high above the clouds beyond.
Oh, how I wonder about that magical place
They call space.

Misha Crossley-Moses (9)
Oakington Manor Primary School, Wembley

Spaceships

Spaceships are so amazing,
They can take you everywhere,
They can take you anywhere,
They can take you where you want to play.

I'm so glad I have this spaceship,
I can ride it anywhere,
I will never lose it.

Zayan Dana (10)
Oakington Manor Primary School, Wembley

Galaxies Of The World

G limmering, shiny stars shivering
A utomatically bright every night
L ight and bright galaxies
A lways shiny and starry
'X tremely beautiful
Y ou will be amazed!

Miracle Oluebubechi Austin-Akuma (10)

Oakington Manor Primary School, Wembley

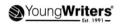

YOUNG WRITERS INFORMATION

We hope you have enjoyed reading this book – and that you will continue to in the coming years.

If you're a young writer who enjoys reading and creative writing, or the parent of an enthusiastic poet or story writer, do visit our website **www.youngwriters.co.uk**. Here you will find free competitions, workshops and games, as well as recommended reads, a poetry glossary and our blog. There's lots to keep budding writers motivated to write!

If you would like to order further copies of this book, or any of our other titles, then please give us a call or order via your online account.

Young Writers
Remus House
Coltsfoot Drive
Peterborough
PE2 9BF
(01733) 890066
info@youngwriters.co.uk

Join in the conversation!
Tips, news, giveaways and much more!

 YoungWritersUK    @YoungWritersCW